HOW IT'S MADE
Shoes

RUTH THOMSON

PHOTOGRAPHY BY CHRIS FAIRCLOUGH

WATTS BOOKS
LONDON • NEW YORK • SYDNEY

© 1993 Watts Books

Watts Books
96 Leonard Street
London
EC2A 4RH

Franklin Watts Australia
14 Mars Road
Lane Cove
NSW 2066

UK ISBN: 0 7496 1348 3

10 9 8 7 6 5 4 3 2 1

Dewey Decimal Classification: 685
A CIP catalogue record for this book is
available from the British Library

Printed in Malaysia

Contents

New trainers	4
Uppers and soles	6
Cutting the uppers	8
Sewing the uppers	10
The tongues	12
The lining	14
Punching lace holes	16
The canvas sock	18
The mould	20
Making the sole	22
The sole	24
Finishing	26
Inspecting	28
Ready to wear	30
Index	32

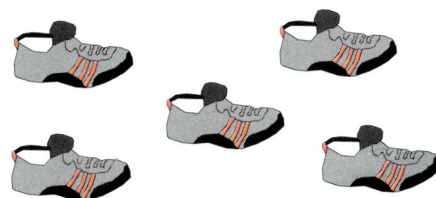

New trainers

Have you ever wondered how a pair of trainers is made?

Twelve pairs, all the same style,
size and fitting, are made
together in a batch.
It takes over five days
to make them.

Guess how many people have a hand
in making them.
You can find out the answer
at the end of the book.

Upper and soles

**Look at your trainers.
They are made of two parts.**

The uppers are the part
that covers your feet.
The soles are the part
you walk on.

These are all the pieces
(except for the sole)
needed for one shoe.
Can you see what each one is?

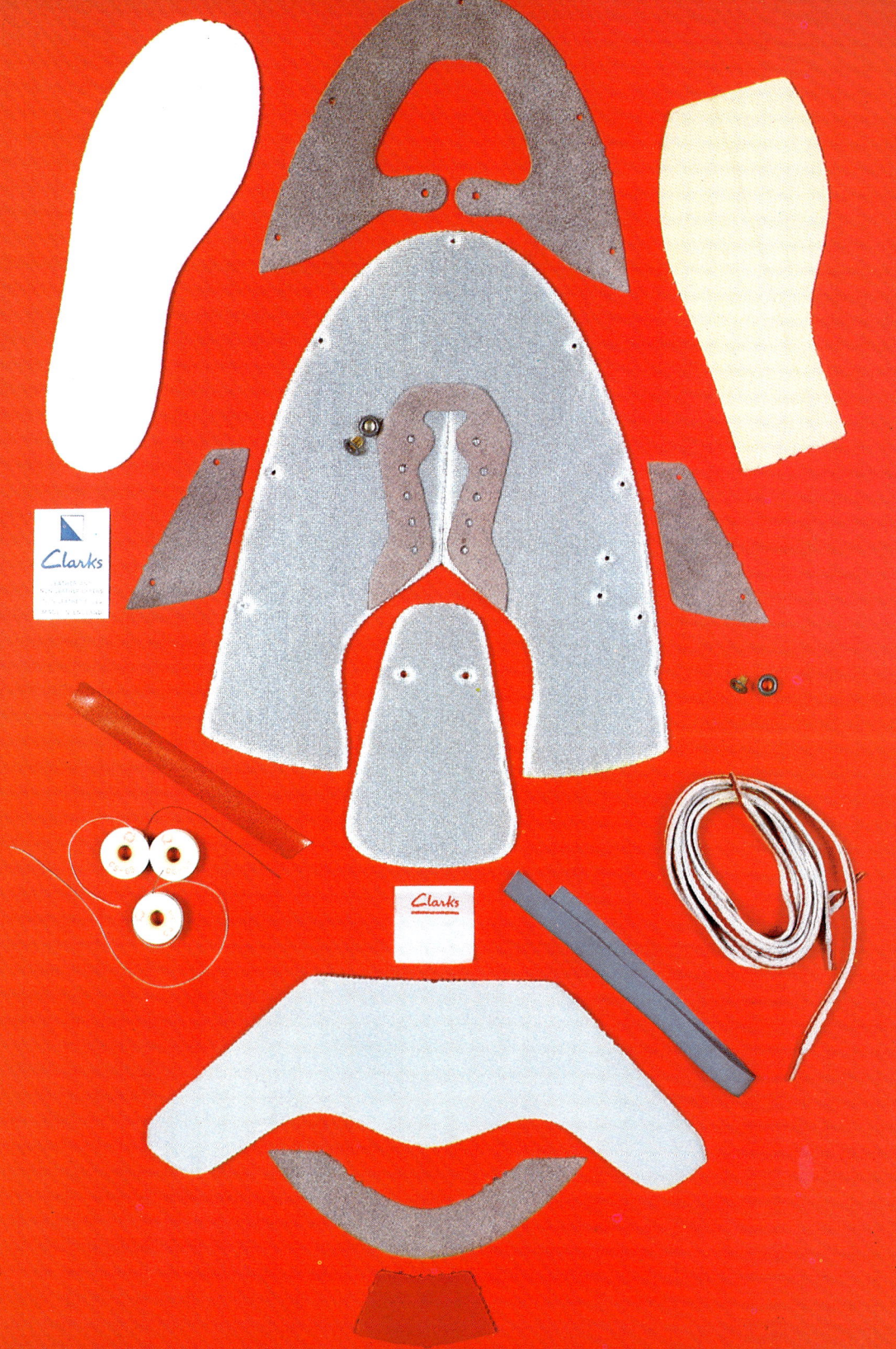

Cutting the uppers

The uppers are made of nylon.

Six pieces are laid on top
of one another.

The cutter puts a knife
on the top piece.
It is the shape of the front
of the shoe.

He moves a big white press
over the knife.
It pushes the knife down and
cuts through all six pieces.

The trimmings are cut separately
from suede.

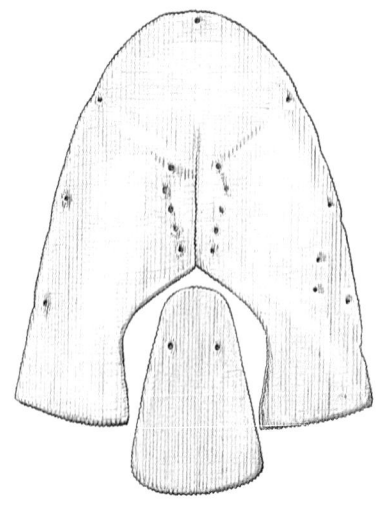

Sewing the uppers

The uppers and trimmings are fitted together in a frame called a pallet.

Can you see the little pins
which hold the pieces in place?

The pallet is locked firmly,
so the pieces cannot move.

It is fixed under an automatic
sewing machine.
This sews the uppers and
the trimmings together.

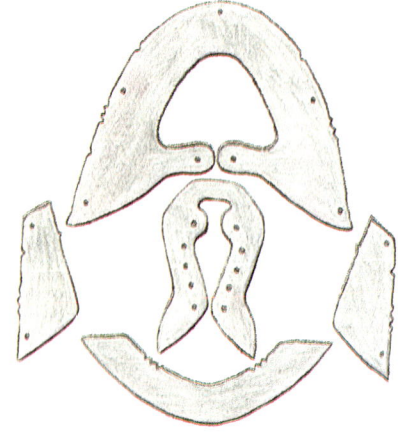

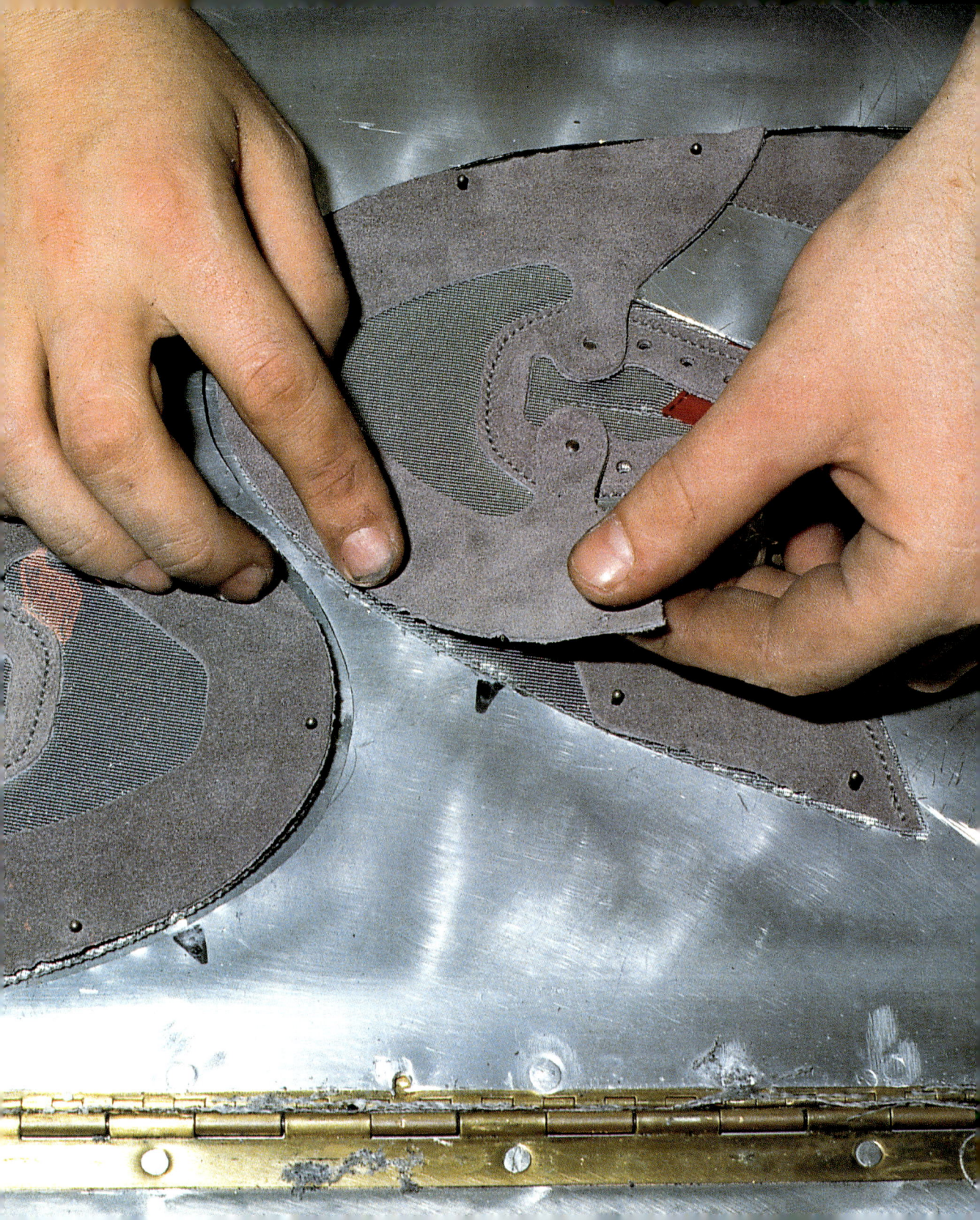

The tongues

The tongues are made separately.

A machinist sews cloth binding
around three edges of the tongue.
This stops it from fraying.

She joins one tongue straight on to
the next.
When she has sewn twenty-four tongues,
she snips between each one
to separate it.

A label with the maker's name
is sewn over the end of the tongue.

Now the tongues are ready to be joined
to the uppers.

The lining

The two ends of the uppers are sewn together and then lined.

The lining is sewn on to the back
of the shoe.
Can you see how the shoe is starting
to take shape in the picture below?

The lining is turned inside the shoe
and stitched in place.
This makes the shoe comfortable
to wear.

Any extra material
is cut away.
Otherwise it might rub
your feet.

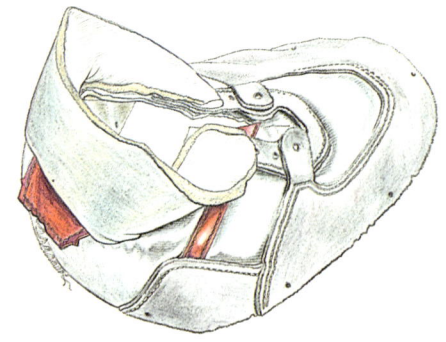

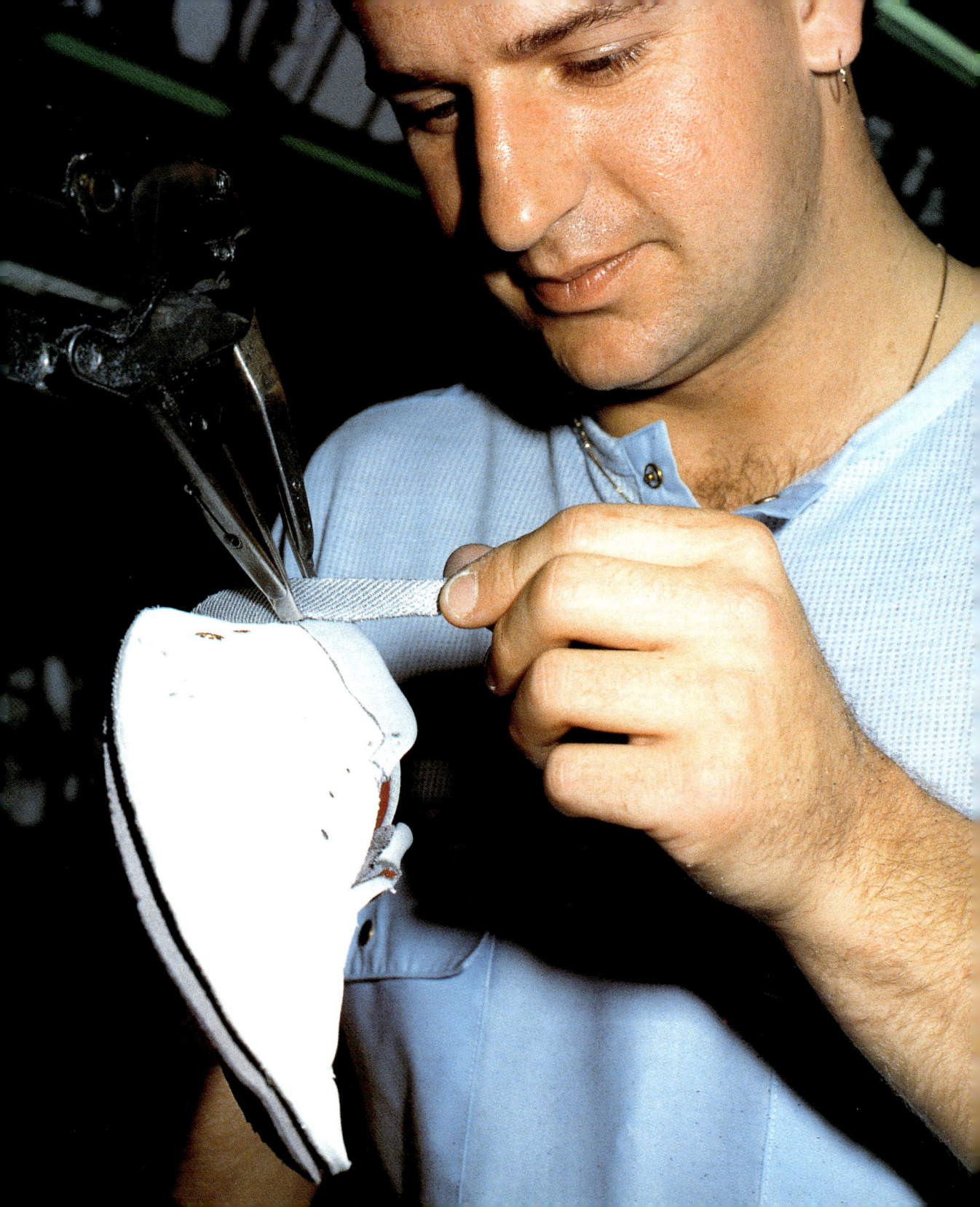

Punching lace holes

Holes are punched for the laces.

Metal eyelets are put on the top
of the two holes to strengthen them.

This machine has just pressed
an eyelet in place.

Can you see another eyelet waiting
to drop over the other hole?

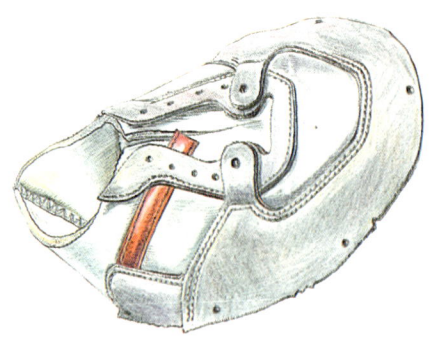

The canvas sock

A canvas sock is sewn on the bottom of each upper.

Can you see the finished sock?

Now the uppers are finished.
They are ready to go
to the moulding room.
Here, the soles will be put on.

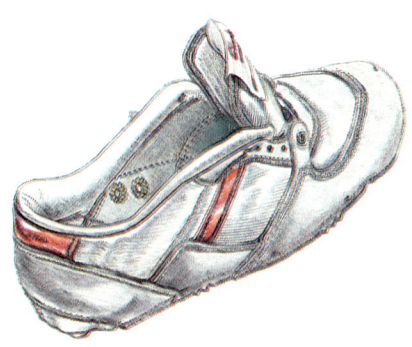

The mould

In the moulding room, the left and right shoes are separated.

The correct size mould for the shoes
is fitted into a mould box.
What size is this one?
The mould has three pieces –
two side pieces and a sole.

The blue foot shape above the mould
is called a last.

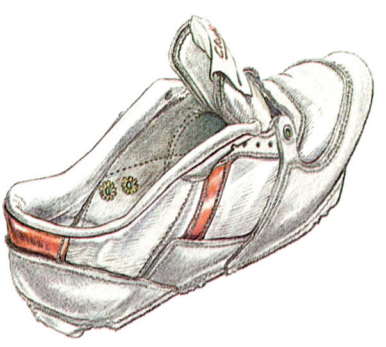

Making the sole

The machine operator puts a shoe over the last.

He lowers it into an open mould.
The shoe is fitted at the front.
Can you see how?
Then the mould is closed.

A hot, sticky mixture is squirted
through a hole into the mould.
It sticks to the rough canvas sock
and the suede trimmings.

The sole

After six minutes, the mixture sets hard and the mould is opened to lift out the last.

Now the shoe has a sole.
Can you see the pattern
of the mould printed on it?

The ragged edges are trimmed
with a knife to make them smooth.

Finishing

A foam sock and a sticky label are put inside each shoe.

The label gives the name
of the shoe makers.
It also gives the country
where the shoes were made.

A finisher snips off
any loose threads.
He cuts off any extra material.
He sponges away any dirty marks.
He buffs the suede with a brush.

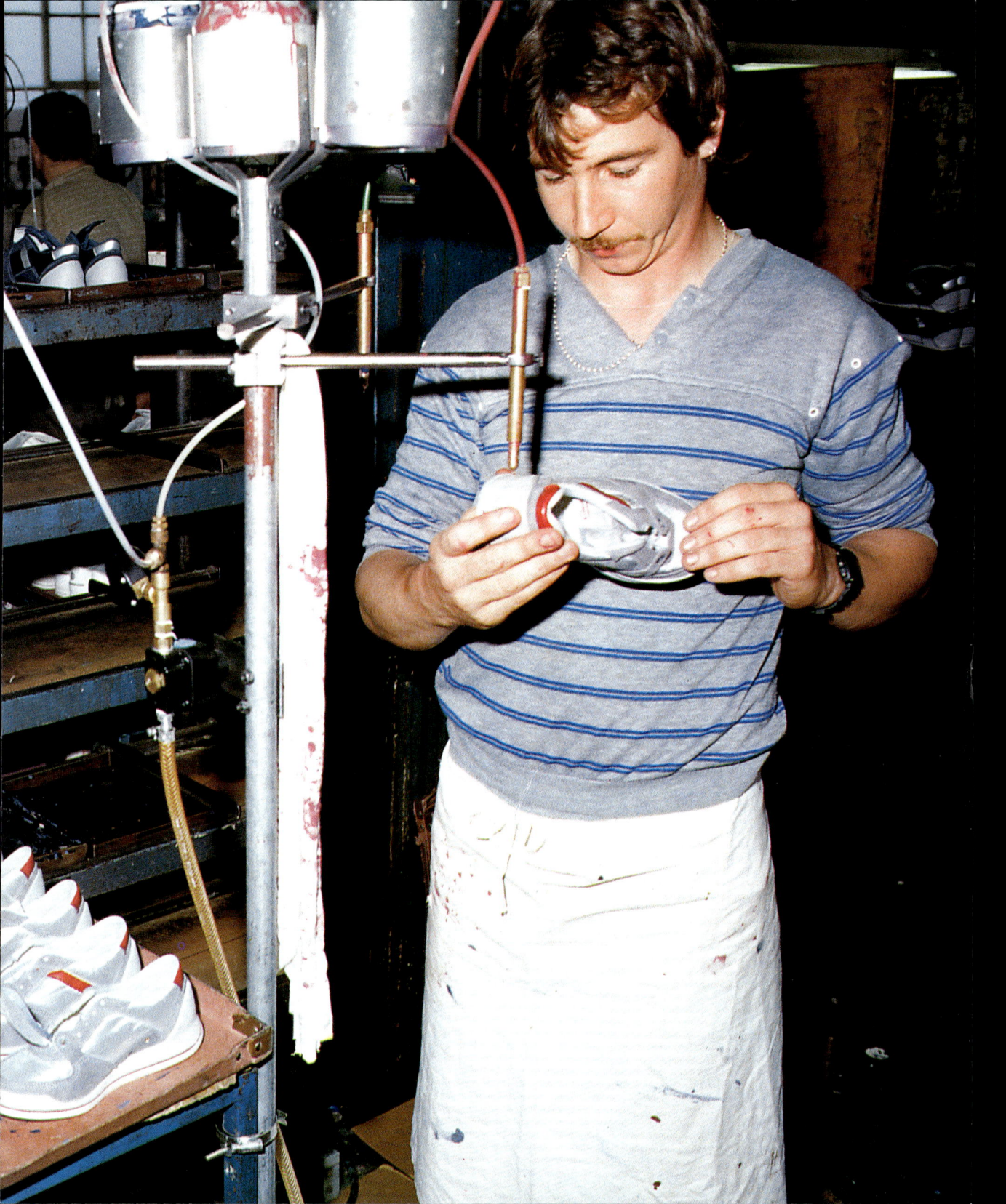

Inspecting

An inspector examines every pair.

He makes sure the colours match.
He looks to see if any stitching
is missing.
He checks whether there are
any dirty marks.

If the shoes pass his test,
they go to the packing department.

Ready to wear

**The shoes are folded in tissue
and put in a box
with a pair of laces.**

The label on the box gives
the style and size of the shoes.

The shoes are sent to a shoeshop,
ready to be bought.

Can you believe it?
More than twenty-five people have
worked on every single pair like this.
Remember this, next time you go
to choose a new pair of trainers.

Index

Box 30

Cloth binding 12
Cutter 8

Eyelets 16

Finisher 26
Fitting 4

Inspector 28

Label 12, 26, 30
Laces 30
Lace holes 16
Last 20, 24
Lining 14

Machinist 12, 14
Machine operator 22
Moulding room 18
Mould 20, 22, 24

Mould box 20, 22

Nylon 8

Packing department 28
Pallet 10
Press 8

Sewing 10, 12
Sewing machine 10
Shoeshop 30
Size 4, 30
Sock 18, 22, 26
Soles 6, 18, 22, 24
Style 4, 30
Suede 8, 26

Tissue 30
Tongues 12
Trimmings 8, 10, 22

Uppers 6, 8, 10, 12, 18